weblinks

You don't need a computer to use this book. But, for readers who do have access to the Internet, the book provides links to recommended websites which offer additional information and resources on the subject.

You will find weblinks boxes like this on some pages of the book.

weblinks

For more information about Fatboy Slim, go to www.waylinks.co.uk/ 21CentLives/DJsandMCs

waylinks.co.uk

To help you find the recommended websites easily and quickly, weblinks are provided on our own website, **waylinks.co.uk.** These take you straight to the relevant websites and save you typing in the Internet address yourself.

Internet safety

↗ Never give out personal details, which include: your name, address, school, telephone number, email address, password and mobile number.

↗ Do not respond to messages which make you feel uncomfortable – tell an adult.

↗ Do not arrange to meet in person someone you have met on the Internet.

↗ Never send your picture or anything else to an online friend without a parent's or teacher's permission.

↗ If you see anything that worries you, tell an adult.

A note to adults
Internet use by children should be supervised. We recommend that you install filtering software which blocks unsuitable material.

Website content

The weblinks for this book are checked and updated regularly. However, because of the nature of the Internet, the content of a website may change at any time, or a website may close down without notice. While the Publishers regret any inconvenience this may cause readers, they cannot be responsible for the content of any website other than their own.

WAYLAND

21st CENTURY LIVES
DJs AND MCs

Debbie Foy

WAYLAND

First published in 2008 by Wayland

Copyright © Wayland 2008

Wayland Books
338 Euston Road
London NW1 3BH

Wayland Australia
Level 17/207 Kent Street
Sydney NSW 2000

The right of Debbie Foy to be identified as the author of the work has been asserted by her in accordance with the Copyright, Designs and Patents Act 1988.

Editor: Claire Shanahan
Designer: Fiona Grant
Design: Peter Bailey for Proof Books
Cover Design: Hodder Children's Books

British Library Cataloguing in Publication Data
 Foy, Debbie
   DJs and MCs. - (21st Century Lives)
   1. Disc jockeys - Biography - Juvenile literature
   I. Title
   791.4'43

ISBN 978 0 7502 5242 3

Cover: MCs Eminem and Busta Rhymes perform on stage in LA, USA, in 2006.
Evan Agostini/ImageDirect/Getty Images: 6; Mario Anzuoni/Reuters/Corbis: 8; Steve Appleford/Corbis: title page, 16; Caetano Barreira/Reuters: 4; Mike Blake/Reuters/Corbis: 21; Will Blochinger/Corbis: 9; Stephane Cardinale/People Avenue/Corbis: 20; Chris Davison/courtesy of Judge Jules: 12; Jon Furniss/Getty Images: 5; Frazer Harrison/Getty Images: front cover, 19; Courtesy of Judge Jules: 13; Nancy Kaszerman/ZUMA/Corbis: 10; Paul McConnell/Getty Images: 17; Travis Oscarson/Getty Images: 14; Fred Prouser/Reuters/Corbis: 18; Christophe Russeil/KIPA/Corbis: 7; Mat Szwajkos/Getty Images: 15; Sebastian Willow/AFP/Getty Images: 11.
Every attempt has been made to clear copyright. Should there be any inadvertent omission please apply to the publisher for rectification.

Printed in China

Wayland is a division of Hachette Children's Books, an Hachette Livre UK company.

Contents

Fatboy Slim
The Funk Soul Brother

Fatboy Slim—one of the world's most famous DJs-turned-popstar!

> **I make music for the hips not the head. I try to make people smile and dance, not think about things or educate them.**
>
> **Fatboy Slim**
> *The Guardian,*
> **December 2006**

Also known as: Norman Cook (born Quentin Leo Cook)

Date and place of birth: 31 July 1963, Kent, England

Background: Attended Reigate Grammar School in Surrey where he started a punk fanzine. Began DJing at friends' parties from the age of 15. While studying at Brighton University, he began honing his DJ skills on the Brighton club scene.

His music in a nutshell: 'Big beat' combining hip hop, electro-funk, breakbeat, rock, house and R&B (rhythm & blues). His 'everything-but-the-kitchen-sink' approach to music includes sampling famous songs to use in his remixes. Irresistibly catchy, toe-tapping, good-time party anthems.

Biggest hits/remixes: *Rockafeller Skank* (1998), *Brimful of Asha* with Cornershop (1998), *Praise You* (1999), *Right Here, Right Now* (1999), *Slash Dot Dash* (2004), *I See You Baby* with Groove Armada (2004), *That Old Pair of Jeans* (2006).

Famous collaborations: Macy Gray, Damon Albarn.

Awards and achievements: A Grammy Award for Best Short Form Video (for *Weapon of Choice*), plus five Grammy nominations. Nine MTV video awards and 13 Top 40 singles. Brit Awards for Best British Dance Act in 1999 and 2001. Fatboy Slim remixes have been used in popular advertising campaigns, including Groove Armada's *I See You Baby* for Renault Clio.

Something you might not know about him: Norman Cook is a shareholder of Brighton & Hove Albion football club, the team he has supported since moving to Brighton in the 1980s.

On the beach at Brighton, where Fatboy hosts his infamous Big Beach Boutique gigs to thousands of fans.

Fatboy Slim is a DJ superstar. Though he cannot sing and does not write lyrics, Norman Cook is also one of the hottest pop stars on the planet. He has achieved stratospheric success by bringing dance music out of the clubs and into our living rooms, entertaining club kids to suburban mums with his infectious samples, catchy beats and his remarkable ear for a great party tune. His spectacular sell-out gigs to crowds often reaching hundreds of thousands, from the beaches of Brighton and Rio to music festivals like Glastonbury and Woodstock, have defined him as a global DJ phenomenon who is truly leading from the front.

Cook's music career began in the 80s with indie-pop band The Housemartins. The band had a number 1 hit, but not long after Fatboy Slim moved to Brighton to pursue his real love: dance music. There he formed Beats International and another number 1 followed in 1990 with *Dub Be Good to Me* – drawing on reggae-style samples from punk band The Clash and 70s soul band S.O.S Band. It was this mixture of styles that earned him the reputation of a musical innovator.

But it was the phenomenally successful 1997 album *Better Living Through Chemistry* that really catapulted Cook into the big time. Full of catchy retro samples, the album produced the Top 40 UK hit *Everybody Needs a 303* and Cook's career went global. After his remix of Cornershop's *Brimful of Asha* stormed to number 1, he was approached by musical heavyweights such as U2, Madonna and Robbie Williams – all wanting him to produce for them.

Cook's 1998 album *You've Come a Long Way, Baby* featured the major hit singles *The Rockerfeller Skank*, *Gangster Trippin'* and *Praise You*. The video for *Praise You*, directed by offbeat movie director Spike Jonze, was voted 'Best Video of All Time' by MTV UK viewers.

A further Grammy award-winning video for *Weapon of Choice* featured a jaw-dropping dance display by Hollywood actor Christopher Walken.

In spite of a hectic schedule, in 1999 Cook married radio and TV presenter Zoe Ball. A year later they had a son, Woody. Whether or not the increased media attention affected his work, Cook's 2005 album *Palookaville* moved away from his sample-based music to more conventional songs with real instruments, including Top 40 hits *Slash Dot Dash* and *The Joker*.

Cook's open-air concerts are legendary, featuring enormous video screens, 3-D lighting and firework displays. Unfortunately, in 2002, police were forced to stop the Big Beach Boutique gig for safety reasons. It was not until 1st January 2007 that Cook was given permission to host Big Beach Boutique 3, a hugely successful gig that he performed to a 'locals-only' audience.

Whether Fatboy Slim is creating groundbreaking videos, chart-topping remixes or performing spectacular DJ gigs in New York, Denver, Rio or Brighton, he has 'come a long way, baby'.

"It is a celebration of the last decade as much as it is a Greatest Hits collection. Over 18 tracks, including ten UK Top 20 singles, a couple of UK number ones and two exclusive new tracks – *Champion Sound* and *That Old Pair of Jeans* – it will lead you down memory lane, before grabbing you by the shoulders and hurling you towards the dancefloor."

Review of the 2006 album *Why Try Harder*, by Astralwerks, Fatboy Slim's New York record label

weblinks

For more information about Fatboy Slim, go to
www.waylinks.co.uk/ 21CentLives/DJsandMCs

Carl Cox
The Ambassador of Dance

DJ Carl Cox played the open air SW4 concert on Clapham Common, London, in 2005.

❝I used to hijack my parents' collection of 70s soul records and get the whole family grooving around the lounge! I guess the early signs were there – my passion for music combined with an over-whelming desire to entertain as many people as possible.❞

Carl Cox on his early memories of wanting to be a DJ
The Evening Standard,
March 2004

Also known as: The 'Three-Deck Wizard'

Date and place of birth: 29 July 1962, Lancashire, England

Background: Left school with few qualifications. Went to college to train as an electrician, but left after six months to pursue a full-time career in DJing.

His music in a nutshell: A crowd-pleasing blend of uplifting hard house and Euro techno.

Biggest hits/remixes: *I Want You Forever* (1992), *Two Paintings and a Drum* (1996), *Sensual Sophis-ti-cat* (1996).

Famous collaborations: Fatboy Slim, Roni Size from Reprazent, Saffron from Republica.

Awards and achievements: *Top of the Pops* appearance in 1996 and awarded International Dance Award for DJ of the Year in 1995 and 1996. Voted by KISS 100 FM DJ Mixer of the Year in 2006. Acting roles in films *Human Traffic* (1999) and *LA DJ* (2004).

Something you might not know about him: Carl Cox saw the dawn of the year 2000 twice. First, he played a 12 o'clock party in Australia's Bondi Pavilion, then hopped on a jet across the timeline to Hawaii to play in the millennium!

Carl Cox is a DJ, a gentleman and a diplomat. Known for his friendly, outgoing personality and his energetic, party-pleasing blend of house and techno, Cox is one of the few DJs around who plays both commercial and underground clubs. He is an acid house veteran, a DJ legend who is regarded by his legions of fans the world over as the ambassador of dance and techno.

Cox grew up with music. His Barbadian parents loved soul and eight-year-old Carl enjoyed spinning singles to get the whole family dancing. By the age of 10, Cox was spending all his pocket money on records, and at 15 he acquired his first pair of decks and began working as a mobile DJ at parties and weddings.

In the beginning, he played soul, hip hop and disco, but in summer 1988 (known as 'the summer of love') Cox began to build his reputation on the acid house scene. It was a midsummer all-night rave that launched his career, when at 10.30am the next morning, he tempted 15,000 weary ravers back onto their feet by hooking up a third turntable to his decks. Cox mesmerised the crowd with his turntable magic – mixing and scratching it up in a truly innovative way – and since this time he has been known as the 'Three-Deck Wizard'.

Established as a DJ, Cox turned to producing and in the early 90s signed to DJ Paul Oakenfold's Perfecto Records, resulting in two Top 40 singles and a *Top of the Pops* appearance. In 1996, business-savvy Cox launched his own record label, Worldwide Ultimatum. His first own-label album *At the End of the Cliché* stormed up the UK charts and Cox spent the next few years rocking dance floors across the world, spreading the word on house music and acquiring a global following. In 1999, Cox appeared in the movie *Human Traffic*, adding acting to his list of achievements.

The clubbers' paradise of Ibiza saw the beginning of Cox's successful residency at the famous nightclub Space in 2002, and Cox returns each summer to spin a mix of funk, soul, Latin, jazz and drum & bass. He has contributed many Essential Mixes for Radio 1, but in 2006 Cox led KISS FM's relaunch by bringing his award-winning show Carl Cox Global to the dance radio station. Pulling in a million listeners every weekend, the 'saviour' of KISS FM spins sets inspired by his jaunts in the UK and abroad. These include Cannes Film Festival, Berlin's Love Parade and the Californian music festival, Coachella (in which he played alongside Madonna and Franz Ferdinand), and UK club nights at SLAM, Cream and Ministry of Sound.

Though his CV includes producing, writing, remixing, managing, acting and presenting, Cox has never lost touch with his audience or with the reason he is a DJ: to spin great tunes, to get people on their feet and to host a memorable party. Carl Cox is a musical pioneer, a businessman and an all-round nice guy. In short, he is the ambassador of dance.

"Music-wise the show is unbeatable, showcasing the very biggest DJs, exclusive live performances and new music aired months before anywhere else."

Gavin Kingsley, the Producer of Carl Cox Global radio show, www.4clubbers.net, 2005

weblinks

For more information about Carl Cox, go to
www.waylinks.co.uk/ 21CentLives/DJsandMCs

Paul Oakenfold
Superstar DJ

Paul Oakenfold arrives at the 2007 Grammy Awards held in Los Angeles, USA.

❝ It's a true passion of mine. I don't know how I'm going to stop doing it. I'll probably end up playing in a little bar once a week. ❞

Paul Oakenfold
www.residentadvisor.net, 2006

Also known as: Oakenfold or 'Oakey'

Date and place of birth: 30 August 1963, London, England

Background: His father was in a folk band and as a child, Oakenfold learned to play the piano and spent hours listening to Radio 1. He trained as a chef, but was DJing by the age of 16. He began playing in a basement bar in London's Covent Garden not long after.

His music in a nutshell: Oakenfold is famous for importing 'Balearic'-style house music (from the Spanish island of Ibiza), trance music, and 'Goan' trance (a type of music discovered on the island of Goa, India). He blends these with European house to create his own distinct sound.

Biggest hits/remixes: Happy Mondays' *Wrote for Luck* (1990), U2's *Even Better Than The Real Thing* (1992), *Big Brother* UK TV theme (2000), *Starry Eyed Surprise* – the Capital Radio theme tune (2002), *Faster Kill Pussycat* (2006).

Famous collaborations: Ice Cube, Snoop Dogg, Massive Attack, Nelly Furtado, Tricky, U2, Happy Mondays, Asher D of So Solid Crew, Madonna.

Awards and achievements: Nominated by British Phonographic Industry (BPI) as Best Producer (1990–93), Brit Award Best Producer (1991), Broadcast Music, Inc. (BMI) Film Music award for the sound track to the film *Swordfish* (2002), BMI Pop Award for *Starry Eyed Surprise* (2003), Grammy Award nomination for Best Electronic/Dance Album for *A Lively Mind* (2007).

Something you might not know about him: Oakenfold has produced music for loads of video games, including the James Bond video *Golden Eye: Rogue Agent*, *FIFA*, *Tiger Woods PGA Tour 2003* and Konami's *Dance Dance Revolution* for Xbox.

Oakenfold's gigs are legendary, often comprising elaborate stages, firework displays and light shows.

Paul Oakenfold has to be the DJ success story of our time. Over the last 20 years, he has carved out a dance music career that has placed him firmly at the top of the pile. A fully paid up member of the DJ elite, these days Oakenfold commands huge fees for his gigs, travels by chauffeur-driven limousine and is friends with the stars. In 2002, Oakenfold moved his family to the Hollywood hills to pursue his new venture in composing music for movies – proof beyond doubt of his superstar status.

Oakenfold's career began in the 80s when he worked for a UK record label, his keen ear discovering and signing Jazzy Jeff and the Fresh Prince (AKA Will Smith) among other chart-topping artists. Oakenfold was DJing as well, and in 1987 a trip to Ibiza changed the face of dance music and propelled Oakenfold onto the music scene in a massive way. Oakenfold decided to import the mix of house, soul, Italian disco and alternative music that he had witnessed in the exploding club scene on the Spanish island. This sound was later dubbed the 'Balearic' and, during the late 80s, this groundbreaking style of house music was to rock clubs across the UK. It was around this time that Oakenfold hosted one of England's first major acid house nights at the club Heaven in London's West End, and suddenly his name began to appear on flyers everywhere.

His success reached the ears of the indie group the Happy Mondays who asked him to remix their single *Wrote for Luck*. The resulting track became the indie-dance crossover record of the time, making dance music accessible to many young people and finally helping house music reach the charts. Oakenfold went on to produce their *Pills, Thrills & Bellyaches* album, which became a platinum-seller and was nominated for a Brit Award.

By the mid-90s, dance music had gripped mainstream British radio and culture, and Oakenfold led the new wave of globe-trotting DJs. He remixed several of U2's hits, such as *Even Better Than the Real Thing*, which went higher in the UK chart than U2's original version. Oakenfold also toured with U2 on their historic ZOO TV tour in 1992/93, playing to audiences of up to 90,000, and with Moby on his USA tour in 2001. This was also the year that the theme tune for the hugely popular *Big Brother* UK TV show was released.

With Oakenfold's talent for creating a musical mood and his refusal to stand still, it is not surprising that he has been recruited into the glamorous world of film music. He has produced music for the movies *Swordfish*, *The Matrix Reloaded*, *Collateral*, *The Bourne Identity*, *Planet of the Apes* and *Die Another Day* – for which he remixed the James Bond theme tune. These days, DJ Paul Oakenfold's name is not found on club flyers, but is more likely to be seen on the rolling credits on your movie screen as you eat your popcorn…

"There are but a handful of DJs in the world who attract the fervour and create the excitement that he is capable of provoking in a crowd."

www.sing365.com

weblinks

For more information about Paul Oakenfold, go to
www.waylinks.co.uk/ 21CentLives/DJsandMCs

Missy Elliott
Hip Hop Heroine

Missy Elliott at the premiere of the film Hitch in 2005.

❝ **I'd stand on the side of the road when I was a little girl singing on trash cans. People would roll down their windows saying, 'isn't she cute?'. I had a vivid imagination. I always pretended it was some big stage.** ❞

Missy Elliott
www.hellomagazine.com

Also known as: Missy 'Misdemeanour' Elliott; (real name: Melissa Arnette Elliott)

Date and place of birth: 1 July 1971, Virginia, USA

Background: Missy Elliott was an only child who grew up with her mother (her father had been abusive towards her mother so she left him). Missy would escape into a fantasy world, writing letters to Michael Jackson to ask him to make her a star. She performed endless songs for neighbours on the street outside her house.

Her music in a nutshell: Danceable, catchy hip hop with an edge. Her lyrics can be hard-hitting and tackle sensitive issues such as sex and relationships.

Biggest hits/remixes: *The Rain* (1997), *Get Ur Freak On* (2001), *Work It* (2002), *Lose Control* (2005).

Famous collaborations: Janet Jackson, Christina Aguilera, Justin Timberlake, Nelly Furtado and Destiny's Child.

Awards and achievements: Brit Award nominations for Best International Female Solo Artist in 2004 and 2006. Grammy Award for Best Female Rap Solo Performance for *Work It* in 2004. Grammy Award nominations for Best Rap Song for *Lose Control* and for Best Album for *The Cookbook* in 2006. Best R&B Song for *Free Yourself*; Best Rap/Sung Collaboration for *1,2 Step*; Best Short Form Video for *Lose Control*. MTV Video Music Awards Best Hip Hop Video and Best Dance Video for *Lose Control* in 2005.

Something you might not know about her: She is the spokesperson for 'Break The Cycle', a charity organisation that seeks to end domestic violence.

She is the queen of MCs, a hip hop heroine and the most successful female rap artist of all time. A talented songwriter, her lyrics are hard-hitting and in-yer-face. She is a positive role model for women and, on her journey to fame and fortune, has shaken up the sound of hip hop and changed the stereotyped ideas of women in rap. She is an icon of our time. She is Missy Elliott.

Missy's musical career began in the late 80s as a member of the girl group Sista. Sista's record label fell through, but Missy's ability to write lyrics, sing and rap soon landed her a record deal. In 1997, her first platinum album *Supa Dupa Fly* hit the streets. Hip hop fans sat up and took notice; Missy Elliott was on the map.

Missy Elliott performs on stage in Berlin, Germany, in 2006.

Until Missy arrived on the scene, female rappers (such as Lil' Kim and Foxy Brown) were stereotyped as glamorous and seductive, but downtrodden, and regarded as sex symbols instead of musical artists. In her early career, Missy defied these stereotypes with her cropped hair, rounded figure and baggy tracksuits. Her outrageous lyrics on songs such as *She's a Bitch* and *Hot Boyz* tackled relationships between men and women, and music industry stereotypes head on.

In 1999, Missy wrote, produced and appeared on former Spice Girl Melanie B's debut solo single, *I Want You Back*, which went straight to number 1 in the UK charts. Her third platinum album, *Miss E ... So Addictive* (2001), produced the massive hit *Get Ur Freak On*. Her next album, *Under Construction* (2002), included *Work It* – Missy's biggest hit to date. This album became the bestselling female rap album ever, with 4.5 million copies sold worldwide.

Over the years, Missy has racked up a star-studded list of musical collaborations, but everyone wants a piece of Missy. In 2003, she starred alongside Madonna in an advert for Gap – proving beyond doubt that she is an icon of our time. When Adidas asked her to produce a range of clothing, shoes and accessories, the range Respect M.E. was born. Then, in 2006, Universal Pictures announced plans for Missy to star in a screen version of her life story. The as-yet unnamed movie is to be produced by actor Robert De Niro.

From fly girl to music mogul, record producer to movie star, Missy Elliott has got it going on...

"A fusion of inventive instrumentals, dynamic and diverse deliveries, and creatively constructed musical movements... the Virginia native continues into her trademark uncharted territory."

Atlantic Records, on Missy Elliott's multi award-winning 2006 album *The Cookbook*

weblinks

For more information about Missy Elliott, go to
**www.waylinks.co.uk/
21CentLives/DJsandMCs**

Judge Jules
The People's DJ

Judge Jules – DJ, broadcaster, promoter and charity campaigner – one of the hardest working DJs of today.

"I'm lucky enough to travel a lot. Some weeks the work-life balance seems just right, whereas there are occasional 7-day periods when I wonder what possessed me to take on board such a silly schedule."

Judge Jules' weekly tour diary, www.judgejules.net, May 2007

Also known as: The Judge (real name: Julius O'Riordan)

Date and place of birth: 26 October 1965, London, England

Background: Attended a north London comprehensive where he followed the punk and New Romantic movements. At the age of 16, he moved to the prestigious University College public school, then went on to study for a law degree at the London School of Economics.

His music in a nutshell: His sets comprise a variety of musical styles with an emphasis on funky, hard house and trance.

Biggest hits/remixes: *Pitchin' (In Every Direction)* (2000), *So Special* (2005), *I Can Hear Voices/Caned & Unable, You & Me, Gonna Work It Out, Ordinary Day* (2006), *Without Love* (2007).

Famous collaborations: Boy George.

Awards and achievements: Smirnoff Dance Award for Best Radio DJ in 2000 and 2001. BBM Award for Best International DJ in 2000, 2001 and 2003. Ranked in the top ten in *DJ Magazine's* Top 100 DJs in 2002 and 2003. M8 Ibiza Dance Awards for Best Ibiza Trance DJ in 2006.

Something you might not know about him: Jules avoids taking his job too seriously; in the past he has reacted against the idea of the 'superstar DJ' by playing the trumpet over his records!

Judge Jules plays at a Tenerife nightclub as part of his summer tour in 2007.

promotes and hosts his multi award-winning Ibiza club night 'Judgement Sunday @ Eden' throughout the summer season.

Jules also produces with friend Paul Masterton under the name Hi-Gate. Hi-Gate performed their single *Pitchin' (in Every Direction)* on *Top of the Pops* in 2000 and several Top 20 hits followed. During his varied career, Jules has produced and remixed many top-selling compilations including numerous albums for the famous London club The Ministry of Sound, and in 2006 he produced an acclaimed compilation entitled *The Global Warm up Mix* and his first solo album and DVD *Proven Worldwide*.

He also finds time in his busy schedule to support Shelter, the charity that helps homeless people, and Cancer Research UK. Jules is also involved with Radio 1 charity fundraising events such as Comic Relief.

Judge Jules can rock dance floors the world over, from the smallest club to largest festival, and he has a posse of devoted followers. It is his hard work, enthusiasm and his dedicated service to dance music that has earned him the title of 'the People's DJ'.

Surely Judge Jules leads one of the busiest lives in dance music? With gigs around the globe, homes in London and Ibiza (a base for his hugely successful club nights on the paradise island), not to mention his producing, charity and TV work. Oh, and of course his regular Saturday night slot on Radio 1. At the peak of his profession, the DJ veteran juggles it all admirably — and has done for over 20 years.

While still at university in the mid 80s, Jules began to host parties with Norman Jay, a popular soul and funk DJ. The events grew in popularity and in 1987 Jules joined the then-pirate radio station Kiss FM. It was around this time that Jules also began to DJ on the London club scene.

As the 90s approached, Jules threw himself into the acid house scene, promoting many of the successful raves that were held around this time. Kiss FM became legal in 1990 and Jules was given two prime weekend slots, often playing to 250,000 listeners. His popularity grew and by the time Jules was invited to join Radio 1 in 1997, he was already a seasoned crowd-puller, playing many top UK club nights and festivals.

Currently Jules plays the Radio 1 Saturday Warm Up, 7–9pm, a show popular with clubbers preparing to go out. One of the most listened to dance radio shows in the UK, it also reaches a worldwide audience due to Radio 1's online and satellite connections. Jules also

> "Jules' ability to pull a crowd, swirl them around and leave them wanting more makes him a club promoter's dream."
>
> BBC Radio 1 website

weblinks

For more information about Judge Jules, go to
www.waylinks.co.uk/ 21CentLives/DJsandMCs

Paul Van Dyk
The DJ Politician

Paul Van Dyk scooped three awards at the American Dance Music Awards in 2004.

66 **If I can use my own exposure to make people slightly more aware of certain issues that cannot be a bad thing.** 99

Van Dyk on using his music to express his political views

Also known as: PvD

Date and place of birth:
16 December 1971, Berlin, Germany

Background: Grew up in the communist state of East Berlin. Captivated by the music of The Smiths and New Order, he recorded that and early house music via radio stations broadcasting from beyond the Berlin wall.

His music in a nutshell:
Immaculately blended trance music – a fusion of techno and house. Trance is repetitious, with a faster beat than house music, and involves the use of synthesizers. Van Dyk plays an uplifting style of trance, including many popular club anthems.

Biggest hits/remixes: *For An Angel* (1998), *Tell Me Why* (2000), *Nothing But You, Time Of Our Lives* (2003).

Famous collaborations: Sarah Cracknell from the band St Etienne, the rock band Vega 4.

Awards and achievements: Grammy Award nomination for Best Electronic/Dance Album for Reflections in 2006. BPM magazine award for America's Favourite DJ in 2004. Trance Award for Best Global DJ in 2006. Voted by *DJ Magazine* Number 1 DJ in 2006.

Something you might not know about him: In 2006, Van Dyk was presented with one of Germany's most prestigious awards – Berlin's medal of honour – for his charity work in support of under-privileged children.

Paul Van Dyk is a DJ with a mission. Though he did not attend clubs or raves in his youth, Van Dyk has established himself as one of the most influential club DJs in the world. His influence, however, does not end with music, as Van Dyk's political ideas are apparent in his work. Though he spends his time travelling the globe playing his upbeat trance sounds to happy crowds, Van Dyk's feet are firmly on the ground.

The superstar DJ signs autographs for fans after performing in New York's Central Park, 2006.

As a teenager living behind the Berlin wall, Van Dyk heard his first house and electronic music via a forbidden West Berlin radio show, or from the occasional tape that was smuggled over the wall into East Berlin. In the absence of a club culture, Van Dyk and his friends taped the music and played it at their parties. When the Berlin wall came down in 1989, Van Dyk was 18 and already had a great knowledge of dance music. He began DJing in Berlin and soon moved on to clubs in the UK and New York.

Van Dyk had had hits before, but it was his *Seven Ways* album in 1998 that established him as a pioneer of trance music. Suddenly, his diary was full with gigs all over the world. In 2003, he released *Global* – a CD/DVD package that captured the sights and sounds of being a global superstar DJ travelling the world, and in 2005 he released *Politics of Dance 2*.

Politics and dance music may not seem to have much in common, but Van Dyk's childhood in East Berlin has taught him that the radio is a window on the world and its music is a route to freedom in certain societies. Van Dyk uses dance music and its youth culture to voice his political opinions, whether it be his opposition to the war in Iraq or playing in the 2004 'Rock the Vote' campaign leading up to the USA's presidential election. There he played alongside Bono, Mary J. Blige and the Black Eyed Peas with the aim to encourage young people to cast their vote. Van Dyk is also the patron of the Indian charity Akanksha that helps children living in poverty.

Van Dyk is known for his stand against drugs, particularly the harmful drug often associated with clubbing known as 'ecstasy' or 'E'. During his residency at famous Sheffield club Gatecrasher, Van Dyk's followers wore t-shirts featuring the slogan 'No E, Pure PvD'.

One of the world's greatest electronic artists, Van Dyk is not content with being simply a superstar DJ – he is keeping it real as a political figure for our generation. PvD for President…?

"An epic journey into uplifting atmospheric dancefloor dreaminess… it's Van Dyk at his best, perfectly chosen, perfectly mixed."

David Jeffries, reviewing the album *Politics of Dance 2*, All Music Guide, 2005

Lady Sovereign
The Big Midget

Lady Sovereign on tour in the USA in 2007.

66 If your heart is in it then go for it man, and don't give up, but just be ready to tackle things that will come in your way. **99**

Lady Sovereign on getting into the music industry, www.ilikemusic.com, 2006

Also known as: Sovereign or Sov (real name: Louise Amanda Harman)

Date and place of birth: 19 December 1985, London, England

Background: Grew up on a tough London estate. Her mother inspired her interest in rap music through the 80s hip hop bands Salt-N-Pepa and The Beastie Boys.

Her music in a nutshell: Rap music featuring witty, Brit-focused rhymes boldly delivered in a strong London accent. Her sound embraces garage, jungle, raga, R&B, ska and punk.

Biggest hits/remixes: *Little Bit of Shhh!*, *Ch Ching*, The Street's *Fit But You Know It* (2004), *Random* (2005), *Nine2Five* – The Ordinary Boys vs Lady Sovereign, *Love Me or Hate Me* (2006).

Famous collaborations: Mike Skinner of The Streets, Missy Elliott, Dizzee Rascal, The Beastie Boys, Basement Jaxx, The Ordinary Boys.

Awards and achievements: Lady Sovereign is the first non-American female ever to be signed to the famous hip hop recording label Def Jam Records.

Something you might not know about her: At the age of 11, Lady Sovereign had soccer trials for Arsenal Ladies team.

The feisty South London rapper performs in Sydney, Australia, 2007.

Cheeky, outspoken and way in-yer-face, this pint-sized MC's lyrical delivery packs a punch. Her music expresses a voice of British urban youth that is rarely heard and her passion for sportswear and trademark side ponytail sets her apart from many female recording artists. Though her witty, quick-fire lyrics are full of true Brit name checks like hoodies and shepherds pie, Lady Sovereign has already won over some of the biggest and best producers in the USA. Make way for the S-O-V…

Sovereign grew up on Chalkhill Estate, one of London's most notorious housing areas. As a teenager, she played truant from school, preferring to write song lyrics than homework. She sold doughnuts and double-glazing for a living, but in her spare time she continued to write songs and post them on the Internet. A product of 90s youth culture and technology, Sovereign's music career was assisted through blogs and forums, which helped build her fan base long before she had even released a song.

In her late teens she landed an acting role in an educational film, ironically about the life of a young MC, and persuaded the producers to let her write the film soundtrack. The record producer Medasyn heard the demo tapes and things were never the same again for Sovereign.

In 2004, her first solo recordings, *Little Bit of Shhh!* and *Ch Ching,* received widespread support and Radio 1 coverage. But it was her appearance on The Streets' *Fit But You Know It* that caught the ear of Def Jam record label boss, Jay-Z. In August 2005, he flew Sovereign to the States, and signed her after she dropped some spontaneous lyrics during their meeting.

In May 2006, she featured on the remix of The Ordinary Boys' *Nine2Five*, which shot to number 6 in the UK Top 40 – her highest chart position to date. Later that year, Sovereign released her debut album *Public Warning* to great acclaim, and these days her diary is packed with dates for festivals and appearances. She also supported Gwen Stefani on her 2007 Sweet Escape Tour.

Sovereign's fashion statement is expressed through her Adidas sportswear and her lyrics speak out against posing in bikinis, fake tan and flowery dresses. But the recent shopping precinct bans on hooded sweatshirts or 'hoodies' prompted Sovereign to visit 10 Downing Street to promote the 'Save the Hoodie' campaign. At just over 1.5 metres (5 feet), Sovereign is the self-confessed 'big midget', but there is nothing small about her success. From council estate girl to cross-Atlantic hip hop star, Lady Sovereign reigns supreme…

"One of Britain's most hotly tipped musicians."

The Guardian, August 2005

weblinks

For more information about Lady Sovereign, go to **www.waylinks.co.uk/ 21CentLives/DJsandMCs**

Eminem

The Rap Phenomenon

Eminem accepting yet another award—this time at the Hip Hop Awards ceremony in California, USA.

"Anybody with a sense of humour is going to put on my album and laugh from beginning to end."

Eminem on his music
www.theeminemwebsite.com

Also known as: Slim Shady, Marshall Mathers (real name: Marshall Bruce Mathers III)

Date and place of birth: 17 October 1972, Missouri, USA

Background: Eminem came from a broken family and moved around with his mother to several trailer parks (caravan sites) before settling in Detroit at the age of 12. By the age of 13, he had developed an interest in rap and begun to perform. At the age of 17, he dropped out of high school having failed ninth grade (Year 9) three times.

His music in a nutshell: Catchy, hard-edged rap, featuring autobiographical lyrics that are sometimes aggressive and violent.

Biggest hits/remixes: *My Name Is, Stan* (2000), *The Real Slim Shady* (2001), *Lose Yourself, Without Me* (2004).

Famous collaborations: Dr Dre, 50 Cent, Elton John.

Awards and achievements: Grammy Awards for Best Rap Album for *The Slim Shady LP* and Best Rap Solo Performance for *My Name Is* in 1999. Brit Awards for Best International Male Solo Artist and Best International Album for *The Eminem Show* in 2003. Grammy Award for Best Rap Album for *The Eminem Show* in 2003. Academy Award for Best Movie Theme Song for *Lose Yourself* from the movie *8 Mile* in 2003. Grammy Awards for Best Male Rap Solo Performance & Best Rap Song for *Lose Yourself* for 2004. Brit Award for Best International Solo Artist in 2005.

Something you might not know about him: Eminem has married and divorced his wife twice! In 1999, he married his high school sweetheart Kim Scott. They divorced in 2001, but then remarried in January 2006. However, they filed for divorce again three months later.

Eminem is a rap phenomenon. The biggest selling artist of our time, he has sold around 70 million albums worldwide. The blonde-haired, blue-eyed rapper from Kansas is responsible for hip hop's cross over into mainstream America. One of the most controversial rappers of our time, his appeal to white, middle class, suburban teenagers has made rap a commercial force to be reckoned with. So will the real Eminem please stand up…?

At the age of 14, Eminem was a huge hip hop fan and MC'ed in a local band called Motor City Duo Soul Intent. At that time, he was called M&M (after Marshall Mathers), but later renamed himself Eminem. As a white rapper, he stood out from the crowd and was often put down, but producer Dr Dre saw an opportunity and signed Eminem to his record label. *The Slim Shady LP* was released in February 1999 featuring *My Name Is* – one of Eminem's earliest hits.

Slim Shady – an invented character who features in several of Eminem songs – is widely regarded as Eminem's 'alter-ego'. Shady is an angry, violent and disillusioned character and through Shady or as himself, Eminem has succeeded in stirring up huge amounts of controversy. His lyrics have been widely criticised as sexist, violent or homophobic (against gay people).

In 2000, *The Marshall Mathers LP* sold over 1.5 million copies in the first week of its release and is known as the fastest-selling rap album in history. It included the huge hit singles *The Real Slim Shady* and *Stan*, featuring a sample from Dido's hit *Thank You*.

The Eminem Show became the bestselling album of 2002 and gave rise to the controversial singles *Cleanin' Out My Closet* and *Without Me*. In the same year, Eminem starred in a semi-autobiographical film called 8 Mile about an angry young rapper from Detroit who uses hip hop to propel himself from his dismal home life. He recorded *Lose Yourself* for the soundtrack and it became the first rap song to win an Academy Award.

Eminem's family problems are well known, but his 2004 album *Encore* featured the single *Mockingbird* in which he describes his feelings for his daughter, Hailie Jade. The album also poked fun at Michael Jackson and Madonna. Over over the years, he has made many enemies, including Christina Aguilera and Britney Spears.

Eminem and fellow rapper Busta Rhymes performing together in Los Angeles, USA, in 2006.

In December 2005, he released *Curtain Call* – his fifth major album. It went straight to number 1 in the UK charts and represented Eminem's fourth consecutive number 1 album in the USA chart. The album's title gave rise to speculation that Eminem was considering hanging up his mic and retiring from rap, but this has been denied by the man himself.

Though initially held back by his race and background, Eminem has achieved massive cross-cultural success. His lyrics have earned him notoriety and few teenage bedrooms across the world are without an Eminem CD. Despite the controversy surrounding the man and his lyrics, it is impossible to ignore Eminem's immense talent as a musician. Long live Shady!

"I've got a lot of time for Eminem. He writes great lyrics which are way ahead. I don't know him very well, but I have met him and think he's very intelligent."

Composer and songwriter Andrew Lloyd Webber, *Heat* magazine, May 2007

weblinks

For more information about Eminem, go to
www.waylinks.co.uk/ 21CentLives/DJsandMCs

P Diddy
The King of Bling

P Diddy has remained at the forefront of hip hop culture for over a decade.

> **" I don't define myself by the size of my jewellery anymore. "**

P Diddy on his famous 'bling' habit – now a thing of the past

Also known as: Puffy, Puff Daddy, Diddy (real name: Sean John Combs)

Date and place of birth: 4 November 1969, New York City, USA

Background: He was born into a middle-class Harlem household. His father was shot dead in a drugs-related incident when Combs was three years old. His mother worked long hours to afford to relocate the family to a New York suburb and for Combs to attend a private school. He later attended the prestigious Howard University in Washington DC, but left early to pursue a career in music.

His music in a nutshell: Pop-inspired hardcore rap, featuring gritty, urban lyrics combined with catchy, danceable beats. This genre of rap has been criticised for its use of obscenities, as well as sexist, racist and materialistic references.

Biggest hits/remixes: *I'll Be Missing You, It's All About the Benjamins, Been Around the World* (1997), *Let's Get Ill* (2003).

Famous collaborations: Will.i.am from the Black Eyed Peas, Nicole Scherzinger from the Pussycat Dolls, Christina Aguilera, David Bowie, Kanye West.

Awards and achievements: Grammy Awards for Best Rap Performance by a Duo or Group for *I'll Be Missing You* and Best Rap Album for *No Way Out* in 1998. Grammy Award for Best Rap Performance by a Duo or Group for *Shake Ya Tailfeather* in 2004. At the time of writing, P Diddy is the richest hip hop entertainer in the world with an estimated fortune of $350 million.

Something you might not know about him: In 2003, Combs successfully completed the New York City Marathon. In spite of his bad knee, and minimal training he managed to raise $2 million for New York public schools.

P Diddy is a multi-million pound media mogul and one of the richest men in music. He presides over a global empire that includes a successful record label, a production company, a fashion clothing line and a chain of restaurants. He has enjoyed enormous success as a music and TV producer, performer and Broadway actor. Added to this, he has raised millions for children's charities and the New York education system. Over the last decade P Diddy has experienced great success, but many low points too. In spite of this, however, the King of Bling has firmly stamped his mark on mainstream culture.

P Diddy hosts the MTV Video Music Awards in Miami, USA, in 2005.

From a young age, it was clear that Sean Combs had a sharp business mind. As a child he came up with ways of profiting from a newspaper delivery round, and at university he promoted parties and ran an airport shuttle service instead of studying. After two years at university, he left to join a record company. At the tender age of 20, he was promoted to the level of vice president! It was here that he started to produce hits for Mariah Carey, Mary J Blige and Notorious B.I.G (AKA Biggie Smalls).

In 1993, (then known as Puff Daddy) he set up the record company Bad Boy Entertainment. This marked the start of an expanding business dynasty, which was later to become known as Bad Boy Worldwide – a multi-million pound global empire.

Puff Daddy featured in a video for Biggie Smalls' hit *Big Poppa* in 1995, accompanied by bikini-clad women in a jacuzzi. Wealthy and successful, covered with fur, diamonds and gold chains and surrounded by beautiful women was the image that Puff Daddy loved to promote through his music and videos. Unfortunately, the hip hop world also had a darker and violent side.

In 1997, Puff Daddy's bestselling artist, Biggie Smalls, was shot dead in a gang-influenced feud. Puff Daddy responded with a tribute song to Smalls featuring his widow Faith Evans, *I'll Be Missing You* – a hip hop remake of the 1983 hit song by The Police *Every Breathe You Take*. The song went straight to number 1 in the USA, UK and around the world.

Though music had made him millions, the business-savvy Puffy was keen to branch out into other ventures. In the late 90s he opened upmarket restaurants in New York and Atlanta, named Justin's (after his eldest son). He also launched Sean John, a fashion clothing line, and around this time dated the singer Jennifer Lopez.

At the start of the millennium, Puff Daddy announced that he was changing his name to P Diddy and appeared in the movie *Monster's Ball* alongside Halle Berry and Billy Bob Thornton. Since then, he has executively produced and starred in an MTV reality series *Making the Band*, and in 2004 he made his debut acting on the Broadway stage.

In 2006, P Diddy released *Press Play* – his first album in four years – to great acclaim. Producer, rapper, fashion designer, restaurateur, TV and Broadway star and one of the most influential people of this century, long may P Diddy reign as the King of Bling.

"…a highly recommended hip hop release that confirms Diddy's position as a major player once again."

Review of *Press Play*
http://www.indielondon.co.uk, 2006

weblinks

For more information about P Diddy, go to
www.waylinks.co.uk/ 21CentLives/DJsandMCs

Other DJs and MCs

Roger Sanchez

Roger Sanchez is one of the best-known house DJs on the planet. Born in New York, USA, in the late 60s, Sanchez (AKA The S-man) spun his first DJ set at the age of 13 and from then was booked for local parties and weddings.

Sanchez was DJing in clubs and studying to be an architect when his father suggested that he give up his studies to pursue a full-time career in music. It turned out to be wise advice as Sanchez soon found himself playing New York's premier clubs, alongside big name DJs such as David Morales and Danny Tenaglia. Sanchez soon achieved iconic status in the European club scene, but especially on the island of Ibiza where Sanchez has held a successful residency since 2000.

Sanchez is one of the few DJs who has mixed commercialism with credibility – and pulled it off. He has enjoyed a red hot remixing career spanning many musical genres, working with Michael Jackson, Elton John, The Police, Diana Ross and Daft Punk! He has released many albums and DJ compilations and has had two Top 30 singles. In 2000, *I Never Knew* reached number 24 in the UK charts, and in 2001 *Another Chance* stormed in at number 1. In 2004, Sanchez won his first Grammy Award for remixing No Doubt's *Hella Good*.

DJ, producer, remixer extraordinaire, radio broadcaster, actor and break dancer – is there any end to this guy's talents?

Pete Tong

If you had to name the most influential people in the UK dance music scene, Pete Tong's name would feature high on the list. Along with DJ Judge Jules, Pete Tong has made the cross over from club DJ to mainstream radio on the country's most listened to station – Radio 1. Born in 1960 in Kent, Pete Tong grew up listening to funk and soul artists such as James Brown. He began DJing at the age of 15 when he was asked to spin some tunes at a friend's wedding. The DJ bug bit him and, on leaving school, he set up as a full-time mobile DJ. In the 80s, when the dance music culture took off, Pete Tong released many of the most influential house tunes of the time, such as *Baby Wants to Ride* by Jamie Principle and *Tears* by Frankie Knuckles.

In 1991, Pete Tong had his big radio break when he was brought in to host the Radio 1 Essential Selection, Fridays 7–9pm. Nowadays, simply known as Pete Tong, his show is recognised as the official kick-start to the weekend. He also hosts In New Music We Trust and is associated with The Essential Mix.

Pete Tong also has a successful production company and DJs at many prestigious clubs around the world, including his famous Pure Pacha nights at Pacha nightclub in Ibiza. He was the inspiration behind the popular saying and the film *It's All Gone Pete Tong* (cockney rhyming slang for 'wrong') and has composed the music for the films *The Beach* and *24 Hour Party People*. He has a highly successful podcast or 'Tongcast', allowing people to download music from his radio shows onto their MP3 player or computer. From club DJ to Radio 1 jock to innovator, Pete Tong just keeps moving forward.

50 Cent

Curtis James Jackson III overcame his rough-and-tough upbringing to achieve worldwide superstar status. Born in 1975 in Queens, New York, 50 Cent grew up fatherless with a mother who made a living by dealing drugs. When he was 8, his mother was murdered so his grandparents took him in. By the age of 12, he was dealing drugs and was later found carying a gun in school. In his late teens, he served six months in prison.

In 1997, his son was born, which encouraged 50 Cent to refocus his life. Keen to make his name on the hip hop scene, his semi-comic track *How To Rob* described how he would like to relieve many rap artists of their cash and jewellery. It had the desired effect as many big-name rappers responded with their own tracks and 50 Cent was on the map.

In 2000, 50 Cent was shot outside his grandmother's house. He had a painful six-month recovery period and was blacklisted by the recording industry. Refusing to be beaten, he self-released *Guess Who's Back?* Eminem heard the recording and introduced 50 Cent to producer Dr Dre. After signing a $1 million record contract, 50's hit album *Get Rich or Die Tryin'* was released in 2003. The album sold over one million copies in its first week of release making it one of the most successful hip hop debuts in history.

Outside of music, 50 Cent starred in the semi-autobiographical film *Get Rich or Die Tryin'* and is set to star opposite Nicholas Cage in *The Dance*. He has been offered a wealth of merchandising contracts since his rise to fame, and has recently earned millions thanks to a Coca Cola buy-out deal. From zero to hero, 50 Cent has turned his life around – the boy done good…

Lisa Lashes
Lisa Lashes is the undisputed Queen of Hard House and one of the world's biggest and best-known female DJs. In the male-dominated world of superstar DJs, Lisa's gutsy, honest, down-to-earth approach to her profession has earned her the respect of legions of devoted fans. Lisa Lashes (born Lisa Rose-Wyatt) earned her nickname as a young girl due to her extremely long eyelashes – and the name stuck. She is known around the globe for her fun sets and upbeat, arms-in-the-air kind of tracks that make people really want to dance.

She grew up in Coventry in the Midlands where she heard her first hard house tracks at a small Birmingham nightclub. Captivated by the sounds, she borrowed a set of decks from a friend and started buying records from charity shops. She played her first gig at a boat party in 1996 and from there her career took off. Soon, she was playing regular club nights at some of the UK's most prestigious clubs and festivals. In 2003, Lisa launched the hyper-successful Lashed parties on the Spanish island of Ibiza, which she has since taken as far afield as China, Korea, Miami, Australia and Japan. The multi-talented DJ can also turn her hand to producing and has released two of the highest-selling dance compilations in the world, *Hard House Euphoria* (2002) and *Extreme Euphoria Vol 2* (2003). Lisa Lashes is a fabulous DJ and girl-next-door all rolled into one. Have a listen…

Mike Skinner
The Streets' Mike Skinner is the most successful MC in the UK; a 'street poet' with a geezerish line in lyrics, he burst onto the scene in the early 2000s and has remained a key artist of the decade.

Born in 1978, Mike Skinner began playing keyboards at the age of five and, as a teenager, built a recording studio in his bedroom. Whilst working at Burger King, he sent demo tapes to record companies, and in 2000, got his lucky break. *Has it Come To This?* was released under the name The Streets and shot to number 18 in the charts.

Originally a group project, The Streets is now Mike Skinner, the one-man band. Described as the 'authentic voice of British youth', he raps about what he know best – British life and culture. His image and delivery are a million miles from the materialistic, bling-bling style of many MCs in the charts today.

Mike Skinner has had 11 top 30 hits since 2001, including a number 1 with *Dry Your Eyes*, and his debut album *Original Pirate Material* was released to a raft of nominations from the 2002 Brit Awards and the prestigious Mercury Music Prize. His 2006 album *The Hardest Way To Make An Easy Living* debuted at number 1 on the UK album chart. A superstar MC who raps about going down to the pub with his mates and not having a girlfriend? Check out his sounds.

Index

21st Century Lives

Contents of more books in the series:

Supermodels 978 07502 5243 0

Gisele Bündchen
Twiggy
Erin O' Connor
Alek Wek
Kate Moss
Marcus Schenkenberg
Tyra Banks
Lily Cole
Jamie Dornan
Other Supermodels

TV Celebrities 978 07502 5240 9

Ant and Dec
Billie Piper
Simon Cowell
The Osbournes
Fearne Cotton
David Tennant
Catherine Tate
Richard Hammond
Tess Daly and Vernon Kay
Other TV Celebrities

Film Stars 978 07502 4810 5

Johnny Depp
Nicole Kidman
Halle Berry
Tom Cruise
Leonardo DiCaprio
Kate Winslet
Russell Crowe
Will Smith
Keira Knightley
Other Film Stars

Millionaires 978 07502 5042 9

Tom Hadfield
J.K. Rowling
Bill Gates
Ajaz Ahmed
Richard Branson
Elle Macpherson
Steve Jobs
Anita Roddick
Jamie Oliver
Other Millionaires

Motorsports Champions 978 07502 5241 6

Fernando Alonso
Nicky Hayden
Sébastian Loeb
Alejandro Maclean
Danica Patrick
Stéphane Peterhansel
Chad Reed
Valentino Rossi
Lewis Hamilton
Other Motorsports Champions

Footballers 978 07502 5043 6

John Terry
Michael Ballack
Ronaldo
Ronaldinho
Andriy Shevchenko
Thierry Henry
Wayne Rooney
Fabio Cannavaro
Steven Gerrard
Other Footballers

Extreme Sports People 978 07502 5045 0

Katie Brown
David Belle
Ricky Carmichael
Tony Hawk
Mat Hoffman
Gisela Pulido
Kelly Slater
Tanya Streeter
Shaun White
Other Extreme Sports Stars

Pop Groups 978 07502 5044 3

Arctic Monkeys
Coldplay
Black Eyed Peas
Sugababes
Kaiser Chiefs
Gorillaz
McFly
Girls Aloud
Green Day
Other Pop Groups

WAYLAND